Twenty

Party masks

Judy Balchin

Search Press

First published in Great Britain 2010

Search Press Limited
Wellwood, North Farm Road,
Tunbridge Wells, Kent TN2 3DR

Text copyright © Judy Balchin 2010

Photographs by Debbie Patterson at
Search Press Studios

Photographs and design copyright
© Search Press Ltd 2010

ISBN: 978-1-84448-481-2

The Publishers and author can accept no
responsibility for any consequences arising from
the information, advice or instructions given in
this publication.

Suppliers

If you have difficulty in obtaining any of the
materials and equipment mentioned in this book,
then please visit the Search Press website for
details of suppliers: www.searchpress.com

*This book is dedicated to my
beautiful granddaughter, Anna-May.*

The Publisher would like to thank Max Cumings,
Freyja Arthur and Joshua Noble for
appearing in the photographs.

Printed in Malaysia

Contents

Introduction

Over the years I have had great fun creating and decorating masks for parties and special occasions. I love the fact that a simple piece of decorated card can be used to transform your appearance. Masks have been used throughout history to celebrate, transform and entertain. They can be beautiful, scary, sophisticated or just plain silly. If you want to be an alien, a robot warrior, a lion, a witch or a devil, then look no further. You will find masks inspired by African, Aztec, Indian and Egyptian cultures; masks decorated with flowers, butterflies, feathers, patchwork, beads, sequins and leaves; masks for a glitzy party or simply for fun. This book will hopefully inspire and help you to create the perfect mask for your celebration, whether it is an adults' or a children's party. Some of the masks are suitable for either adults or children, and at the end of the book there are some children's masks.

In writing this book I have covered many ways of producing and decorating masks. Plastic sunglasses, paper plates, shaped card and preformed masks are all used and adapted to create the required impact. To make it easier for you, where necessary, mask templates are provided throughout the book to help you

with the construction of the mask base.

So bring out the child in you, along with some paints and a few embellishments…and enjoy the party!

Attaching elastic to your mask

Some preformed masks have been used as a basis for the party masks shown in this book (please see the Search Press website, www.searchpress.com for a list of suppliers). Preformed masks usually come with the elastic already attached. If they don't, or if you are making your own mask from a template in the book, please follow these instructions.

For paper plate and light card masks, a length of round elastic can be stapled to each side of the mask, just above the eyeline. Alternatively, make a small hole on either side of the mask and thread with elastic. Knot the ends of the elastic to secure.

For masks that are heavily decorated or for papier mâché masks, it is best to use stronger flat elastic. Attaching eyelets to the holes will give a more permanent, professional finish.

Eyelets are used for some of the masks.

Preformed full-face and eye masks, which are used to make some of the party masks in this book.

Glittering Butterfly

Materials:

Glitter card

Gold craft stickers: butterflies, leaves
and border

Glue

Gold embroidery thread

Round elastic

2 gold eyelets

Tools:

Scalpel and cutting mat

Pencil

Eyelet setter

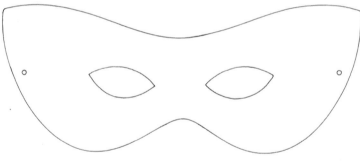

*The template for
this party mask, shown
half the actual size.
Enlarge it 200 per cent
on a photocopier.*

Instructions:

1 Photocopy the template to the correct size and cut round it using scissors. Use the template to help you cut the mask from glitter card with a scalpel and cutting mat.

2 Press the craft sticker border around the edge of the mask and around the eyes, using a scalpel to trim the border to fit.

3 Press eight butterflies and six leaf craft stickers on to glitter card and cut them out using a scalpel and cutting mat. Bend the wings of the butterflies slightly.

4 Cut eight 8cm (3in) lengths of gold embroidery thread and fold them in half. Glue one length, at the fold, to the back of each butterfly so that the cut ends trail below the butterfly body.

5 Attach a gold eyelet to either side of the mask using the eyelet setter. Thread a length of elastic through the eyelets and knot to secure.

6 Glue three leaves to each top edge of the mask and then decorate your mask with the glittering butterflies.

With a mask base cut from glitter card and a few gold peel-off stickers, you too can be the belle of the ball!

Pretty Poppy

Materials:

Preformed eye mask
Red, yellow and black acrylic paint
Black ribbon and sequin trim
Strong glue
Sprig of fabric poppies with leaves

Tools:

Pencil
Scissors
Paintbrush

Instructions:

1 Paint the left side of the eye mask red and the right side yellow, blending the colours in the middle. Allow to dry.

2 Paint a 5mm (¼in) black border around the edge of the mask and a 2mm (⅛in) black border around each eye.

3 Glue the ribbon and sequin trim around the edge of the mask and above each eye.

4 Glue the leaves from the sprig of poppies across the top of the mask.

5 Glue the poppies down the right side.

Vibrant fabric flowers and a decorative ribbon trim are used to decorate this preformed eye mask, creating a theatrical feel.

Exotic Egyptian

Materials:

Paper plate
Blue acrylic paint
Embossing inkpad
Gold and pale blue
  embossing powders
Coloured faceted gems
Glue
Round elastic

Tools:

Pencil
Scissors
Scalpel and cutting mat
Paintbrush
Small piece of sponge
Heat tool
Hole punch

*The template for this party mask,
shown half the actual size. Enlarge it
200 per cent on a photocopier.*

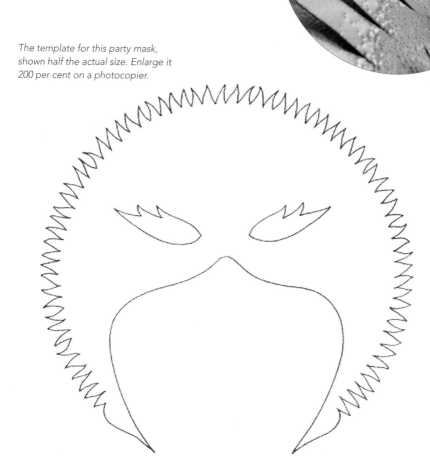

Instructions:

1 Place the plate face down on your work surface. Photocopy the template to the right size, cut it out with scissors and use it to help you draw the areas to be cut out with a pencil. Cut them out using a scalpel and cutting mat.

2 Use the leftover piece of plate to cut the two decorative shapes to sit between the eyes. Paint all the pieces with blue acrylic paint.

3 When this is dry, form a small piece of sponge into a pad, dab it on to the embossing pad and sponge the embossing fluid around the edge of the plate and above each eye hole. Sprinkle with gold embossing powder, remove the excess powder and heat with a heat tool.

4 Sponge an inner border of embossing fluid inside the gold embossing. Sprinkle it with pale blue embossing powder, shake off the excess powder and heat. Decorate the two decorative shapes in the same way.

5 Glue the decorative shapes to the mask and for a final sparkle, glue faceted gems around the edge of the face and the eyes.

6 Using the hole punch, make a small hole at either side of the mask, thread with elastic and knot the ends to secure.

A simple paper plate, decorated with gold embossing and faceted gems, is transformed into this exotic Egyptian mask with a truly regal feel.

Sizzling Devil

Materials:

Red card
Red background paper
Glue
Red and bronze sequins
2 orange eyelets
Round elastic

Tools:

Pencil
Scalpel and cutting mat
Eyelet setter
Wooden spoon

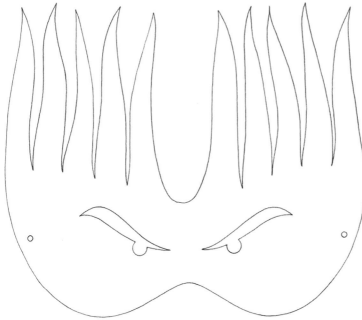

The templates for this party mask, shown half the actual size. Enlarge them 200 per cent on a photocopier.

Instructions:

1 Cover an A4 sheet of red card with red, patterned background paper.

2 Using the main template to help you, cut out the mask shape and pencil in the eyes. Using the smaller template, cut out two eyebrows.

3 Glue two 1.5cm (¾in) diameter circles of red card over the eyes. Draw in the pupils using the template to help you and then cut out the eye shapes using the scalpel and cutting mat.

4 Curl the eyebrows slightly. Spot the inner edges with glue and then press one above each eye.

5 Attach an eyelet to each side of the mask and thread with elastic. Knot the ends of the elastic.

6 Decorate the mask with red and bronze sequins and finally curl the flames round the end of a wooden spoon.

Bring out the devil in you with this sizzling mask decorated with curling paper flames and sequins.

Green Man

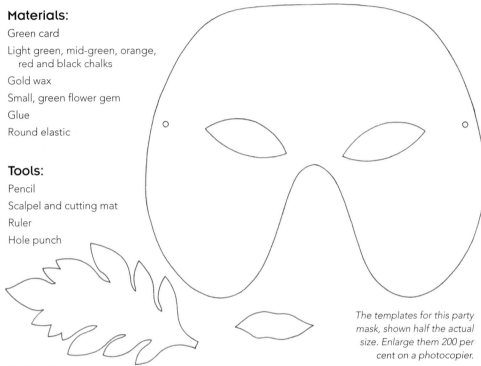

Materials:

Green card

Light green, mid-green, orange,
   red and black chalks

Gold wax

Small, green flower gem

Glue

Round elastic

Tools:

Pencil

Scalpel and cutting mat

Ruler

Hole punch

*The templates for this party
mask, shown half the actual
size. Enlarge them 200 per
cent on a photocopier.*

Instructions:

1 Photocopy the templates to the right size and use them to help you draw
the mask on green card. Cut it out and cut out the eye holes using the scalpel
and cutting mat.

2 Cut thirteen large leaves and seven small leaves from green card.

3 Score down the back of each leaf using the back of a scalpel and
a ruler to create a leaf vein. Bend each leaf slightly.

4 Use the coloured chalks to rub over the leaves. When
they are coloured to your satisfaction, rub a little black
chalk down each score line to highlight the leaf vein and
then rub over them lightly with gold wax.

5 Curl the ends of the leaves slightly round a pencil and
lay them in position round your mask.

6 Glue the thirteen large leaves around the mask,
trimming them to fit around the eye holes. Glue the
smaller leaves in a semicircle between the eyes to hide the
ends of the larger leaves. Glue a flower gem to the centre.

7 Make a hole in either side of the mask, using a hole
punch, and thread with elastic. Knot the ends to secure.

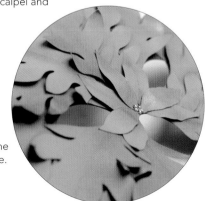

Create your own May Day celebration Green Man mask with a little card and some coloured chalks.

Dazzling Aztec

Materials:

Thick watercolour paper
Tube of gold outliner
Watercolours
2 gold eyelets
Raffia
Round elastic

Tools:

Pencil
Scalpel and cutting mat
Paintbrush
Hole punch
Eyelet setter

The template for this party mask, shown half the actual size. Enlarge it 200 per cent on a photocopier.

Instructions:

1 Photocopy the template to the right size, cut it out and draw round it on watercolour paper. Draw the eyes and nose.

2 Use a pencil to draw in lines, circles and swirls over the mask as shown. Then pipe over these with gold outliner and leave to dry.

3 Fill in all the sections with vibrant watercolours.

4 When dry, decorate areas with dots of gold outliner and leave to dry.

5 Use a scalpel and cutting mat to cut out the mask and the eye holes and cut around the nose.

6 Using a hole punch, make holes around the top edge of the mask. Knot a length of raffia through each hole.

7 Finally use the eyelet setter to attach a gold eyelet to either side of the mask and thread with elastic.

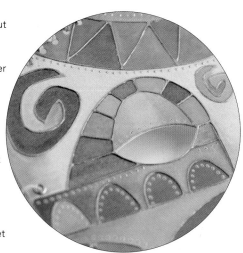

Use your brightest watercolours and gold outliner to create this vibrant
Aztec mask.

Funky Punk

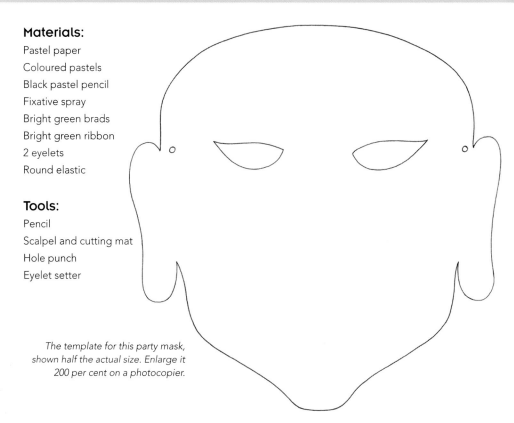

Materials:

Pastel paper
Coloured pastels
Black pastel pencil
Fixative spray
Bright green brads
Bright green ribbon
2 eyelets
Round elastic

Tools:

Pencil
Scalpel and cutting mat
Hole punch
Eyelet setter

The template for this party mask, shown half the actual size. Enlarge it 200 per cent on a photocopier.

Instructions:

1 Photocopy the template to the right size, cut it out and draw round it on pastel paper. Draw the eyes.

2 Colour the face with pastels, blending the colours to achieve a realistic look. Add the eyebrows with a black pastel pencil. Spray the image with fixative to fix the pastels.

3 Use the scalpel and cutting mat to cut out the mask and the eye holes.

4 Decorate the mask with brads to look like piercings.

5 Use a hole punch to punch nine equally spaced holes along the top of the mask and thread them with ribbon as shown.

6 Bend the ears forward slightly. Use the eyelet setter to attach an eyelet to either side of the mask, just above the ears, and thread with elastic. Knot to secure.

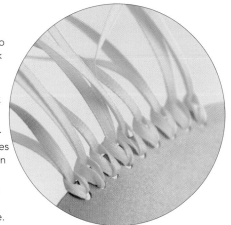

Pastels are used to create this funky face, it is then decorated with vibrant ribbons and brads.

Feather Fantasy

Materials:

Preformed eye mask
Brown acrylic paint
Coral-coloured card
Glue
Coral-coloured sequins
Large brown and coral-
 coloured feathers
Small natural coloured
 feathers
Large decorative sequin

Tools:

Pencil
Scalpel and cutting mat
Ruler
Paintbrush

The template for the beak,
shown full size.

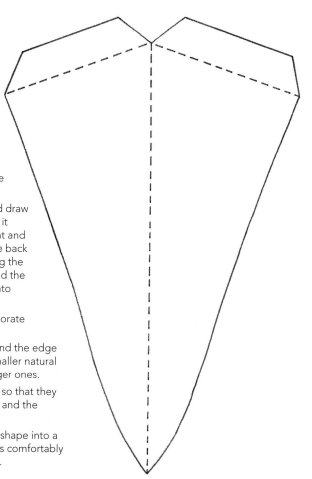

Instructions:

1 Paint the preformed mask with the brown acrylic paint.

2 Photocopy the beak template and draw round it on coral-coloured card. Cut it out using the scalpel and cutting mat and score along the dotted lines with the back of the scalpel and a ruler. Bend along the score lines to create the beak. Spread the flaps with glue and press the beak into position between the eyes.

3 Cover the beak with glue and decorate it with sequins.

4 Glue a row of larger feathers around the edge of the mask. Glue an inner row of smaller natural feathers so that they overlap the larger ones.

5 Glue the smallest natural feathers so that they radiate out from the top of the beak and the eye holes.

6 To hide the feather ends, cut a 'v' shape into a large decorative sequin, so that it sits comfortably over the beak, and glue it into place.

A card beak is attached to this preformed eye mask before it is decorated with natural feathers and sequins. Inset: for a more feminine, subtle look, use pastel-coloured feathers and sequins.

Frosted Flowers

Materials:

Preformed full mask

Cream acrylic paint

Gold leaf and size

Strong glue

Length of gold sequin trim

Sprig of fabric flowers
    with leaves

Tools:

Pencil

Scalpel

Fine sandpaper

Paintbrush

Large soft paintbrush

Hole punch

*The template for this party
mask, shown half the actual size.
Enlarge it 200 per cent
on a photocopier.*

Instructions:

1 Photocopy the template to the right
size and cut it out. Use a pencil to draw
the sections to be removed from the mask,
following the dotted lines on the template.
Cut these away with a scalpel. If the cut
edges are uneven, smooth them with fine sandpaper.

2 Paint the mask with cream acrylic paint.

3 Draw the swirls over the mask to be gold leafed.
Paint these with size using the paintbrush, and when
completely dry, press the gold leaf over the swirls and
press it flat with your fingers. Remove any excess gold
leaf with a large, soft brush.

4 Run a line of strong glue around the edge of the
mask and over each eye. Press sequin lengths on to the
glue and trim to fit.

5 Arrange the leaves around the mask, leaving a gap
for the flowers on the right-hand side of the mask.

6 Use the hole punch to make holes around the left and top edge of the mask and thread the leaf stems through the holes, gluing them on the back of the mask. Glue a few of the leaves on to the front of the mask to secure them.

7 Glue the flowers into place.

This preformed mask is decorated with gold leaf swirls and glittering fabric flowers to create the perfect mask for a fantasy party.

Bhairab

Materials:

Preformed full mask

Strong glue

Large red gem

PVA glue in a bottle with a nozzle

Red and black acrylic paint

Length of decorative trim

Gold wax

Black elastic

Tools:

Pencil

Scalpel and cutting mat

Paintbrush

Hole punch

The templates for this party mask, shown half the actual size. Enlarge them 200 per cent on a photocopier.

Instructions:

1 Photocopy the template to the right size. Using the dotted lines as a guide, draw the areas to be cut from the preformed mask. Use a scalpel to cut these out, including the slits at the sides. Use the waste pieces to cut five small skull shapes.

2 Use strong glue to stick a large gem to the forehead of the mask and then use the bottle of PVA glue to pipe decorative swirls and dots on to the mask. Add the detailing to each skull in the same way using the template to help you. Leave the mask and skulls to dry thoroughly.

3 Paint the mask and skulls with red and black acrylic paints, blending the paints together as you work.

4 Glue a length of decorative trim across the top of the mask and glue the skulls, equally spaced, along the trim.

5 Rub over the mask and skulls with gold wax so that it highlights the dried PVA decoration.

6 Use a hole punch to make a hole in either side of the mask and thread with black elastic. Knot the ends to secure.

Bhairab is known as a fierce manifestation of the Hindu god, Shiva, and Bhairab masks are often found in Nepal, where he is worshipped by Hindus and Buddhists alike. This preformed mask is piped with PVA glue and rubbed over with gold wax to create an ornate finish.

Patchwork Persona

Materials:

Assorted scraps of fabric

Preformed full mask

PVA glue

Coloured buttons

Strong glue

Coloured ribbons, sequin trims
    and strips of fabric

Black elastic

Tools:

Scissors

Paintbrush

Scalpel

Hole punch

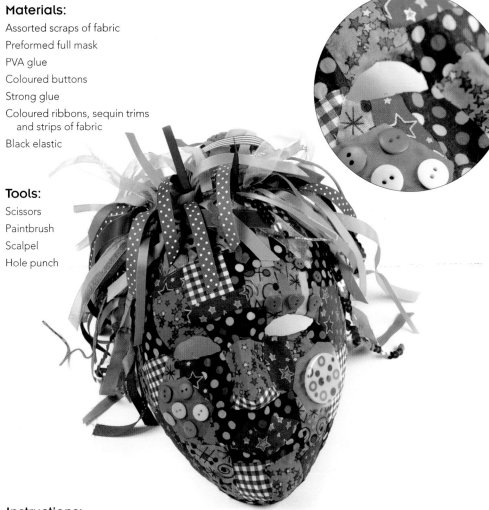

Instructions:

1 Cut squares and rectangles of different coloured fabric. Soak them in a mixture of half PVA glue and half water for a few seconds and then press them on to the mask, overlapping the pieces to create a patchwork effect.

2 Cut two irregular shapes for the cheeks and a lip shape. Paste these on top of the patchwork. Leave to dry.

3 Decorate the mask with coloured buttons, stuck on with strong glue.

4 Use a scalpel to cut small slits on each side of the mask and across the forehead where the hair will go.

5 Push lengths of ribbon, sequins and strips of fabric through the slits and secure them on the inside of the mask with glue.

6 Use a hole punch to make a hole on either side of the mask and thread with elastic. Knot the ends of the elastic to secure.

Search your craft boxes for scraps of fabric, ribbons and buttons to create this vibrant patchwork mask.

African Metal

Materials:

Large sheet of textured
   watercolour paper

Grey watercolour paint

Glue

Gold wax

Square metallic brads

Raffia

Wooden stick

Sticky tape

Tools:

Paintbrush

Scalpel and cutting mat

Ruler

Hole punch

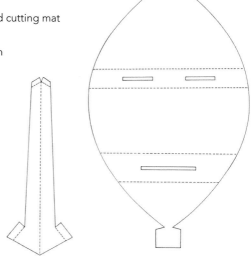

The templates for this party mask, shown a quarter of the actual size. Enlarge them 400 per cent on a photocopier.

Instructions:

1 Paint the watercolour paper randomly with grey paint. When dry, cut the outer mask shape, using the template to help you, with the scalpel and cutting mat.

2 Using the remaining grey watercolour paper, cut one 2 x 18cm (¾ x 7in) strip for the eyes, one 3 x 16cm (1¼ x 6¼in) strip for the mouth, three small strips for the teeth and twenty-one small triangles. Cut out the nose shape using the template to help you.

3 Glue the strips into place across the eyes and the mouth and cut the eye and mouth slits. Attach the teeth across the mouth slit. Glue the triangle shapes to the mask and trim off any overhanging card pieces.

4 Score the nose shape along the dotted lines using the back of a scalpel and a ruler. Fold and glue the flaps and attach the nose to the mask.

5 Rub over the mask with gold wax to give it a metallic look and decorate it with metallic brads.

6 Use a hole punch to make holes down each side of the nose at the top of the mask and thread with pieces of raffia.

7 Glue and tape the stick down the centre of the back of the mask. Wrap the flap at the bottom of the mask around the stick and glue to secure. Finally wrap the stick with lengths of raffia, knotting them to secure.

To evoke an African theme, a basic shield shape is used for this mask. Textured paper is painted and rubbed over with metallic wax to give a metallic sheen.

Seashell Secret

Materials:

Watercolour paper

PVA glue

Blue and turquoise tissue paper

Strong glue

Small shells and starfish

Yellow craft seaweed

Blue and turquoise ribbons

Watercolour paints: burnt
   umber, cadmium orange and
   cadmium yellow

Three bronze-coloured eyelets

Wooden stick

Tools:

Scalpel and cutting mat

Paintbrush

Eyelet setter

The templates for this party mask, shown at half the actual size. Enlarge them 200 per cent on a photocopier.

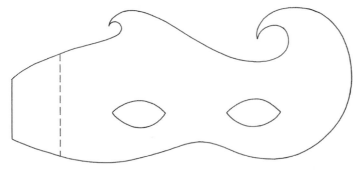

Instructions:

1 Photocopy the templates to the right size and cut them out. Draw round them on watercolour paper and cut out the mask. Leaving the left flap undecorated, paint the front of the mask with a mixture of half PVA glue and half water. Use a brush to paste torn pieces of coloured tissue paper over the mask until it is covered.

2 Use strong glue to stick a row of shells along the bottom of the mask and two starfish between the eye holes.

3 Glue seaweed around the shells to create the sea bed.

4 Using the template to help you, cut the boat from watercolour paper. Draw and cut out some seagull shapes. Paint the boat with watercolours. Use the eyelet setter to attach eyelets for the portholes. Glue it to the top of the mask. Glue the seagulls around the boat.

5 Apply some glue to the top 6cm (2³/₈in) of the stick. Wrap the undecorated flap around the stick so that 1cm (³/₈in) of the top of the stick is visible above the mask.

6 Glue a shell to the top of the stick and then tie ribbons around the space between the shell and the mask.

Create a few waves at your next fancy dress party with this easy-to make sea-themed stick mask.

Scary Witch

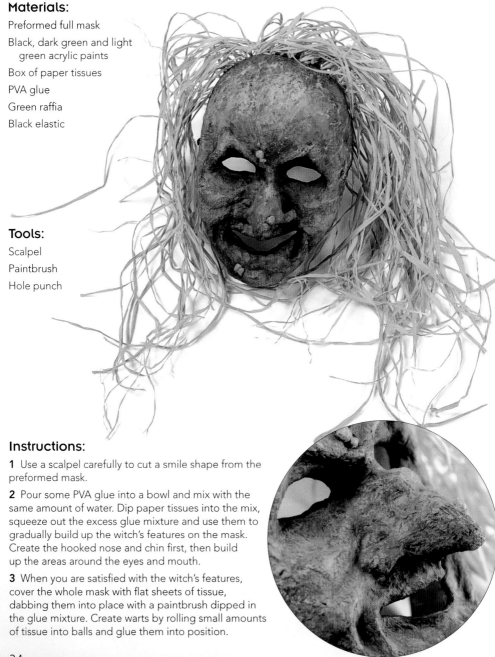

Materials:

Preformed full mask

Black, dark green and light green acrylic paints

Box of paper tissues

PVA glue

Green raffia

Black elastic

Tools:

Scalpel

Paintbrush

Hole punch

Instructions:

1 Use a scalpel carefully to cut a smile shape from the preformed mask.

2 Pour some PVA glue into a bowl and mix with the same amount of water. Dip paper tissues into the mix, squeeze out the excess glue mixture and use them to gradually build up the witch's features on the mask. Create the hooked nose and chin first, then build up the areas around the eyes and mouth.

3 When you are satisfied with the witch's features, cover the whole mask with flat sheets of tissue, dabbing them into place with a paintbrush dipped in the glue mixture. Create warts by rolling small amounts of tissue into balls and glue them into position.

4 Put the mask in a warm, dry place to dry for around twenty-four hours, then, paint it with dark green acrylic paint. Darken the areas around the eyes and mouth with black acrylic paint and then rub over the mask with light green paint.

5 Punch holes around 1cm (³/₈in) apart where the witch's hair will grow. Thread a long length of green raffia through a hole from the front to the back of the mask, then thread it back to the front through the nearest hole. Continue in this way to create a full head of hair.

6 Punch a hole in either side of the mask and thread with strong elastic. Knot the ends of the elastic to secure.

Easy to make paper pulp is used to build up the features of this witch on a preformed full mask. It is then painted and threaded with raffia hair. The smaller version uses a preformed eye mask and the same technique.

Lilac Fairy

Materials:

Preformed eye mask
Metallic lilac and purple acrylic paints
Pink feathers
Sprig of pink wired beads
Glue
Lilac and white paper flowers
White fabric flowers
Large and small round lilac gems
Small lilac and pink flower gems

Tools:

Paintbrush

Instructions:

1 Paint the preformed eye mask with lilac paint, and when dry, paint the border around the edge of the mask and round the eyes with purple paint.

2 Glue two feathers to either side of the mask.

3 Glue wired beads to the mask so that the beads splay out from the edge of the mask.

4 Decorate the mask with paper and fabric flowers, layering the smaller flowers on top of the larger ones and bending the petals upwards to give a three-dimensional look.

5 Glue a large gem to the centre of each large flower, a small gem to the medium sized flowers and a small flower gem to the small flowers.

6 Glue a row of small pink flower gems around the top of each eye hole.

Create a little magic with this lilac fairy mask. The preformed mask is painted with metallic paint and embellished with feathers, paper flowers and gems.

Glamorous Pumpkin

Materials:

Preformed eye mask

Yellow, orange and red acrylic paints

Glue

Bronze-coloured sequins

Gold border sticker

Green card

Green seed beads

Tools:

Scalpel and cutting mat

Paintbrush

The template for the stalk, shown full size.

Instructions:

1 Carefully cut the eye holes of the preformed mask into large triangle shapes, using a scalpel. Cut a smaller triangle for the nose.

2 Paint the mask orange and then blend in yellow stripes radiating out from the top. When this is dry, paint the border round the edge of the mask in red.

3 Glue a row of sequins round each eye and the nose. Glue radiating lines of sequins down the orange sections of the mask.

4 Press strips of gold border sticker around the edge of the mask.

5 Cut two stalk shapes from green card. Cover one shape with glue and drop seed beads on to the glue, arranging them to completely cover the card.

6 Glue the top 3cm (1¼in) of the two stalks together, leaving two flaps at the bottom. Slip the flaps over the top of the mask with the beaded stalk at the front. Glue the flaps to the mask.

Have a happy Halloween party night with this beaded and sequined pumpkin mask.

Robot Warrior

Materials:

Beige and maroon card

Brown and rust-
    coloured inkpads

Gold wax

Metallic brads

Metallic eyelets

Copper-coloured wire

Round elastic

Tools:

Scalpel and cutting mat

Pencil

Eyelet setter

Sticky tape

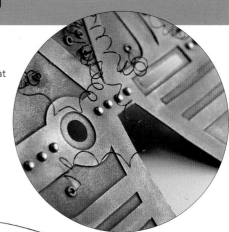

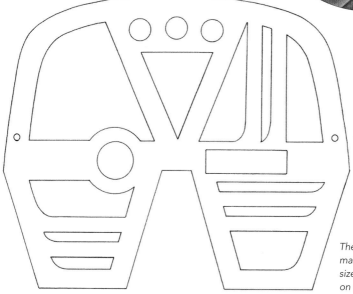

*The template for this party
mask, shown half the actual
size. Enlarge it 200 per cent
on a photocopier.*

Instructions:

1 Photocopy the template to the right size, cut it out and draw round it on beige card.
Using a scalpel and cutting mat, cut it out and glue it to a sheet of maroon card.

2 Still using the scalpel and cutting mat, cut off the excess maroon card and cut a 1cm
(³⁄₈in) diameter hole for the right eye and a 0.5 x 3.5cm (¼ x 1.5in) slit for the left eye.

3 Use the brown and rust-coloured inkpads to rub over the mask to achieve a mottled,
aged look and then rub over the mask lightly with gold wax to give a metallic sheen.

4 Decorate the mask with lines of metallic brads, to look like rivets.

5 Use the eyelet setter to attach six eyelets to the forehead triangle shape and six
more randomly spaced over the upper half of the mask.

6 Spiral six lengths of wire around a pencil and thread each wire from an eyelet in the triangle to one of the outer eyelets. Secure the wire ends with tape on the back of the mask.

7 Attach an eyelet to either side of the mask and thread with elastic.

Card is cut and layered and threaded with spirals of wire to create this futuristic Robot Warrior mask.

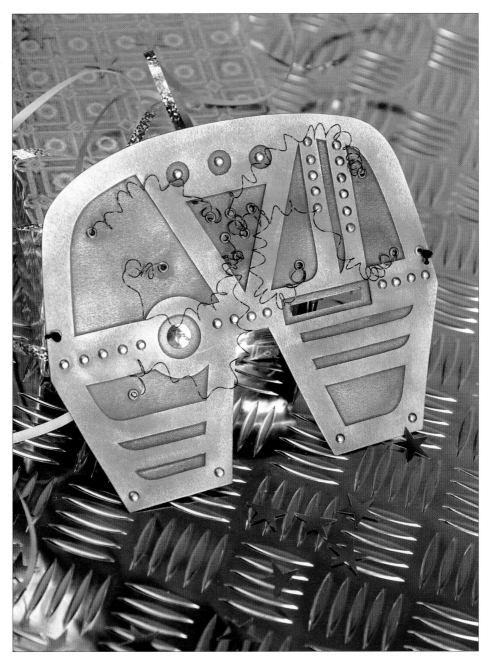

41

Glitzy Glasses

Materials:
Sheet of purple funky foam

Plastic sunglasses

Glue

Foam flower and circle shapes

Tools:
Scissors

Pencil

Scalpel and cutting mat

The template for this party mask, shown half the actual size. Enlarge it 200 per cent on a photocopier.

Instructions:

1 Photocopy the template to the correct size and cut round it using scissors. Cut out the eyes holes. Lay the template on to a sheet of foam, draw round it with a pencil and cut out the foam mask using a scalpel and cutting mat.

2 Lay the folded sunglasses so that the lenses lay over the eye holes. Use a pencil to mark the foam on either side of the mask at the hinge points of the sunglasses.

3 Use the scalpel and cutting mat to cut two slots in the foam big enough to take the arms of the glasses.

4 Lightly draw round the sunglasses with a pencil.

5 Remove the glasses and glue foam flowers and circles to the area outside the pencilled line.

6 When dry, slip the arms of the glasses through the slots.

Try putting on the glitz with these sparkling masks created with a sheet of foam and some plastic glasses. For the green version, foam heart shapes and glittering gems are used to create the perfect Valentine's party mask.

Crazy Alien

Materials:

Paper plate

Acrylic paints: green, purple and white

Coloured pompoms

5 pink chenille stems

Round elastic

Tools:

Scissors

Pencil

Paintbrush

Glue

Sticky tape

Hole punch

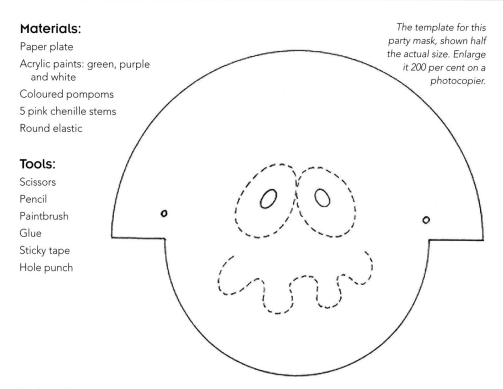

The template for this party mask, shown half the actual size. Enlarge it 200 per cent on a photocopier.

Instructions:

Tip Work on the back of the plate. To help support the plate while painting, place it on top of two blank paper plates.

1 Using the template to help you, cut away the bottom rim of the plate and remove it. Use a pencil to draw in the eyes and then cut out the two eye holes.

2 Paint the plate with green paint and the eyeballs white. When dry, paint purple spots over the centre part of the plate.

3 Glue a large pompom to the plate for the nose. Bend a pink chenille stem into a wiggly mouth shape and glue it below the nose. Glue a pompom to each end of the mouth.

4 To make the antennae, twist two chenille stems tightly together to create a strong stem. Spiral the stem around your finger and glue a pompom to the end. Make two.

5 Glue or tape the antennae to the back of the mask.

6 Decorate the top rim of the mask with pompoms.

7 Use a hole punch to make a small hole in either side of the mask, thread with elastic and knot the ends.

A paper plate can be transformed into a funky alien with some paint, a few chenille stems and lots of colourful pompoms.

Sparkly Lion

Materials:

Paper plate

Cream, black, yellow, orange and red
  acrylic paints

Orange sequins

Glue

Round elastic

Tools:

Pencil

Paintbrush

Scissors

Hole punch

*The template for this party mask, shown half the
actual size. Enlarge it 200 per cent on a photocopier.*

Instructions:

1 Cut out the mask shape and eyes from the paper plate using the template to help you. Do not cut the slits for the lion's mane yet.

2 Use a pencil to draw in the lion's nose, cheek pads and curling decorations following the dotted lines on the template.

3 Paint the lion with acrylic paints.

4 Turn the plate over to the back and paint a 5cm (2in) orange border around the edge. When dry, cut slits around the edge of the plate to create the mane.

5 Curl the strips around a pencil.

6 Decorate the mask with sequins.

7 Use a hole punch to make a small hole at either side of the mask, just within the mane, thread with elastic and knot the ends.

Cutting and curling the edge of this paper plate mask creates a wonderful mane for your paper plate lion.

You are invited to visit the
author's website
www.judybalchin.com